D1548049

HEART RISING

POEMS

ILONA SCHENK

ISBN: 979-8-9852343-5-0 (paperback)
        979-8-9852343-7-4 (eBook)

Library of Congress Control Number: 2022902342

Cover designed by Nskvsky
Edited by Andrea Laws and Lori Weaver

First paperback edition June 2022.

Printed in the United States of America

Published by Ilona Schenk
Richmond, Virginia
www.ilonaschenk.com

This book is dedicated
to my Daughters. I love you.

To Mary.

And to you the reader, whom I may never meet in person.

I want you to know that you are in my heart.

Author's Note

When heartbreak enters your life, you find yourself
spinning out of your mind and body. The throes of ago-
nizing pain breaks you wide open. It is an unexpected
death of all you thought you knew. The stability of a
projected future is lost and transformed forever.
Psychologically, spiritually, and physically there are
many reasons why you feel what you feel, but all of that
doesn't matter when you are wondering how you are
going to survive the next moment.

I didn't set out to write this book. The book wrote itself
through the months of healing from my own broken
heart. It was channeled through the raw metal of grief
and the slow but steady insights that came to me along
the way. Pain can be alchemized. The poems carry a
universal truth through which you can reflect upon your
own experience on your unique journey of healing.

I am sharing these words with you, dear reader, as a tes-
timony and guide through the darkness of the soul.

One thing I know for sure: you, too, will come out the
other end with gold.

Note: Switch genders as you wish - hearts break for all.

Contents

(read first & last)

Shattering

Void

I no longer wonder what it
feels like to be
trapped in the void of
now, without the option to
escape.

Broken Words

broken words tore down all

floating fragments of unfinished dreams,
questions held in past memories,
torn away by aching truths
trust couldn't trust

not even Mother.

life disconnected at once
quiet blood pulsating through a
flatlined body
how was I ever going to survive this dying?

The giver of strength saying
nothing, at all.

Kali

toxic patterns brewed
under the surface
long before Kali
ripped her sword
through complicated
entanglements of life.

Making Room

Some volcanoes never
erupt
while others rid
themselves
blowing acid
ashes,
making room.

Grasping

grasping thoughts
insecurities rush in like soldiers
rescuing their dead,
pulling the wounded out of
conflict they didn't choose.

wild beasts come,
siege continues,
devour,
pray.

Tangled

The impossible is
    happening every day.
        The force weighs heavy.

A skyward earthbound tremble
    reality a integrate spider web,
        the last argument tangled.

In this moment, I am a stranger to
    my fingertips, threads of
        identity untethered.

Sometimes

Sometimes what is plain to see
remains invisible.

Sometimes laughter
comes from despair.

Sometimes what comes naturally
takes a lifetime of growth.

Sometimes the stone in the yard
knows more about life than you.

Sometimes a message from the universe
demands attention.

Sometimes what seems to last forever
—ends.

This Love

An ocean of tears,
floods my chest cavity,
    I don't want this love to end.

I remain in the space in-between,
allowing insights to slowly penetrate the
      shore of confusion,

dependable moon kissed tides will
decide, what stays and
    what will go.

Percolating

irritability gnawing my bones
struggling to settle

world in my hands
faintly presenting

its hieroglyphic conversation.
helplessly looking for

solutions.
raging.

maybe do this or
maybe do that.

percolating all
there ever was, is,
will be.

Will I ever trust again?

The Cove

The cove is dry
desert spread to fish
and turtles' homes,
snakes are gone.

Strategic, slow
withering
preparing the land—
kissing this hard moment.

Hopeful,
after the drought,
raindrops drench the
thirsty clay,

life will return.

Container

instead of moving into action
I am held in an intense
stagnation.

with a stiff neck and
tight body of a deer
I freeze, brain grown

incapable of gestating facts
surrounded by
ruminating intrusion.

I ask emotions
to settle safely into
a container of surrender,

instead of doing, I ask time
to hold me open for
undoing.

Creatures

All sorts of creatures hide
mingling below the light,
even when introduced,
maintaining their masks,
yet when I meet them,
they are strangely familiar.

Ilona Schenk

A Home of My Own

I asked,
wanting a home of my own,
"Am I being too extra?"
seeking a sanctuary
where water speaks of hope,

sunshine gently sends its love
eagles windward soar,
a place to leave
earthly belongings,

my body's
form imprinted on
cozy chair fabric where
each fold whispers a story.

A place
without contamination, familiar
walls to unload elemental
burdens spilled on the
walkways of life.

Exposure

Slow fades the
image of how
I used to fit into
this world.

Exposing
the place where
I know nothing, to
rediscover everything.

People

People tell you who they are.

Listen.

People's actions speak louder.

Observe.

People say death can come from a broken heart.

Truth.

Aflame

confused and torn
naked string of emotions,

helpless, unable to grasp
a wick to set aflame.

angered I invite
flaring sadness

drowning heaps of tears
stomping this torched swamp open,

plotting to force relief.
barely standing.

I would have liked to talk about love,
instead its match lit me.

Sanity

I question sanity.

How can reality be so deceiving?

How can love co-exist with lies?

How can this world go on?

Abyss

Still staring at the abyss

between the life lived and
the
wilderness ahead.

Withdrawal

Ilona Schenk

Seeds

Rain for weeks,
cleaning wounds
ruled by blindness
embracing illusion
while seeds grew into trees.

Generational Trauma

Replaying memory,
as hollowness sits right
behind the cords where
bravery resides and

fear demands silence to honor the
chalice filled historical record,
generational trauma disrupt
sound contemplation.

Noticing this moment,
holding space for self
through this desolate place.
allowing grace

to the heavens,
burdens carried,
lives reclaimed,
sacrificed,

ancestry of scorned women
forever in the air, like the
fly catcher in uncle's barn.

How many unsuspecting flies

met their demise on
yellow sticky tape?
Was it inevitable fate,
gluing them right in front of
familiar eyes?

Initiation

it's hard to tell how deeply
shame infiltrated the
casing of a soul until
heartbreak burst open the
seal that held it together,
sheepish conformity to fit in
to be safe carrying life down a
river lined with buoys labeled;
good enough, loved enough,
wanted enough, perfect…
suggesting anchored happiness.
when all floods,
essence seeps through cracks
drowning reason to pretend,
rawness takes all illusion.
trust in self returns,
it must.

Expectations

gripping
a lost future,
surrendering
self-destruction,
coming to realize,
let all expectations go,
false stability
meant nothing
to a life without
self-respect.

Entrust

Wonder what future will bring
Which decisions usher new beginnings.

My heart aches in
lack of unknowing.
My mind chiming
solutions,
always ready to play
the odds at the thousand
possibilities game.

What if control wasn't an illusion?
What if my knowing was right?
What if everything is meant to be?

Again and again,
starved by logic,
emotions controlled,
struggling to settle
in this invisible
universe.

Lost in option filled gutted land

I surrender to love

entrust the heavy lifting,
so this life can live.

Beyond

she gazes
beyond candle lit
altar's bowl of
fresh water

and emotions.
holding a breath,
noticing its pulse can
just be, for now.

diving into
happened events
half her age ago
bargaining for attention.

murky mind,
disappointed spirit,
breaking surface,
exhaling windows open.

song of the birds,
red berries,
solitude of trees,

wrapped fragrance,

then
she remembered why
leaves change, the
motivation of evergreens,

calling of a girl
insistent to see love,
practicing mornings
of each new day.

It Was

It was a simple high.

Not felt in months.

A small crack

where the light came back.

Echo

The undying
newness is fragile.

The heart hasn't grasped
nor fully trusted light
shining through a collapsed past,

stranded in ruins of
beliefs - fragmented self,
never imagined being here.

An echo of hope.

As darkest nights continue
sweeping over quickening breaths,
trapping below everlasting rhythm of
death under life.

As Long as it Takes

chaos erupts in what has
begun to heal,
a thin scab bleeding,
demanding another look
at what forcefully unearthed
leaving a gasping hole
of promised life.

but, you can't pull
a blooming weed
without spirit blowing
dandelion parachutes
against the wind
germinating
as long as it takes.

Ilona Schenk

Tightrope

She is watching anxiety

walk across a tightrope.

She lost herself

in her own

destiny.

Delicate Balance

how does the ocean not
lose its water
uncontrollably flowing to the shore,
how does it contain itself
without losing itself completely?

yet quietly, unnoticed
the sun absorbs
while clouds carry
restoring rain.

how to live this life
unconditionally loving?
a hidden delicate balance
split open.

Tears

Tears hold vigil.
Calling resistance to surrender.

Some days,
she looks to escape the
slow dying of this soul.
Like a nervous stranger
joy has visited with
fading footsteps.
Yearning to reclaim
her rightful place.
Beyond walls of
protective confusion,
true inheritance of being

audition for peace.

Exhale

oh, how I despise
uncertainty.
where will I go?
what if this and that?
I want to move
out of this moment.
maybe grounding
will come,
regardless.
I need this inhale
to let go.

The Night

The night lifts.
Slowly, body appears.
infinite forms
reach out,
escaping
hidden broth anxiety
eager to join morning
promises
of
life's
abundant
invitation
to
feel unhurt
again.

Tired

Moving through molasses,
swimming upstream,
forcibly noticing sweetness
combating a fatigued dream.

Life's Own

her heart continues to chip.
she sits-on her hands,
counts the pieces,
assembles tears,
gluing hope.
freed and done
she hopes to become
life's own work.

Beginning

Reality held together by common
beliefs. Not ready to go deeper
until betrayal cracked her open.

Reenacting trauma, seeking
resolution. Years became mystical
illusions. Centuries begged to

arrive at conclusions. Breaking
shackled patterns of confusion.
Rewriting, returning, rewriting.

Let the past be the road marker,
not a stop sign. A pause
to reinvent, examine, heal.

Freeing all women who
came before, building
liberation for all who follow.

Beginning with her.

A Quarter

A dance wrote his
moves.
Promising what couldn't
be promised.
Abundant musical chairs.
As the music slowed,
steps of mistruths came down.
I stood in-between
white waves of
inaudible sound fragments.
dizzy, no chair,
Holding a quarter
for the jukebox.

Get Up

Get up, little girl.
Don't abandon you.
Darling(s) walk away.
Be sad, enraged, confused.
this is your life, not theirs.
You get to choose.
That's your gift.

Own it bravely.

Moments

life is composed of bullets:
dates jumbling through time,
lover names no longer exist,
achievements come and gone,

failures recognized and let go.
what stands out in recollection of
decades seems like trying to
hold air in the palms of my hand.

it's all elusive.
if it wasn't for the paper
bearing witness,
pictures,
moments of memories,

all would be easily
swallowed in the alchemy of time.

left are shelves filled with
potions of freedom's choice
as wind carries to
new adventures.

No Rainbows

He's a perfect him.
All else is the hurt speaking.
Traits behind a mask,
bringing you to your knees.
Handing you a box of
darkness.

In this place,
kindness weakens the deceit,
deflection distorts the truth,
agreeableness softens the control.
Empathy excuses the
callused heart.

Surviving through dissonance
saving you a thousand times
from walking, speaking,
admitting, surrendering,
breaking
familiar chaos.

Stop clinging to reflection of
projection for self-protection.
Notice confusion.
Stop excusing.
There is no rainbow in
red flags.

You Are the Cosmos

She is made of water.
He drinks it.
Her body glitters with stardust.
He reaches for a broom.

Trick

The cruelest trick
your mind plays
wanting to be held by the
person who hurt you.

Beginning

Before She Let Go

her thoughts clung to her mind.
She stayed up wondering about purpose.
Opinions held her back.
Before she let go, she pushed through,
afraid emotions would unravel her soul.

Tormented before she let go.

She didn't know who to turn to.
She searched internet answers.
She prayed to spirit to deliver insight.
She felt helpless.

Before she let go, she was tired.

Relationships suffocated her,
hands red from holding on.

Before she let go, she let it all be, she

sat down with herself,
let her tears fill the ocean,
allowed fierceness to rise.

She welcomed all past decisions.
Let go of shame and guilt.

Before she let go,
she placed her hand on her heart,
bowing in silence.

Her breath returned.
For the first time,
she smiled.

(inspired by Safire Rose's *She let go*)

Return to Her

Excitement

Excitement fills the air,
a gust of freedom
settles in my bones,
kindling compassion.

A mangled mind at peace.
taking in the scenery
the fog in the valley
the refreshing mist.

Assured, hope
will bargain with fear
through galaxies
until I am home.

Growing

Fear breathes
down your back,
a predator you can't see
relentlessly signaling
that all will end, eventually.

You struggle.
You push.
You denounce solitude.
Stillness reminds you of
the fragility of love.

Life whispers -

Lean in.
Trust.
I will hold you.
Carry you, through
growing invincible wings.

Ilona Schenk

Choices

You have come too far, my love,

to let choices of another

pull you down.

Indestructible

It's o.k. to be scared.

You are better

braver than you were
a moment's passed.

Allow ash dust to settle.
Lava to harden.

Strengthening foundation.
Your path is indestructible.

Pirate Kites

flying pirate kites,
swimming among guppies in the
vastness of her belly
filled with salty life.
seagulls greeted me,
calling with their song—
surprised.
returning home
not knowing I was gone.
feeling her pull,
her energy
unwilling to give up,
forever powerful.
bowing in gratitude,
thankful of the reminder.
held within her
vastness.
Especially now.

Life's Thread

Nature comes together
stripping down
to its rawest form,
decomposing,
renewing vitality,
intentionally moving
closer to the source,
purposefully crafting in
divine time.
Following life's thread.

She Said

The light that shines through you is
the most important point in
the entire universe.

Believe that!
She said.

You Are Whole

On this cold morning,
when birds still sleep and the
bear hasn't been seen for months,
darkness begins to break.

Slowly hope enters from a
dependable morning sun.
Offering solace through the
white linen curtains;

If you only remember one thing, Love,
you have never been less than whole.

Tender(nest)

Become one with grass.

Grow with sun.

Nest with bees.

Gently

You can't push the heart,

but you can
gently encourage
an opening,

telling you to trust.
Leaning into infinite
possibilities

to

choose

anew.

Flaming Heart

Every grain of your being
fundamentally draws you closer
into the flaming heart of Mother,
touching eternity.

Forever here,
forever moving,
she encourages harvesting
soul fire to come towards

your potential,
to reclaim your power,
bow and arrow in hand.
Oh, warrioress!
Welcome!

Blessed are you!

The Healing Process

the healing process
illuminates
droplets of
fear
obligation
guilt.
insights without
witness
ushering clarity.
opening space to
rejoice.
breathing the same air,
expanding
fluid
connection.

Trust

trust your guides will build

this house to be a home.

protected. loved. supported.

She is Waiting

She is waiting with
hot ceremonial cacao.
Welcoming are the

creases of her skin.
Softness streams from
her tenderness.

Close your eyes.
Invitation to fall
into universal embrace.

Reconnecting
sustaining source.
Comfort your heart,

release toxic patterns.
Provide your inner child
nurturing you never received.

Grandmother's Cheeks

My skin is softening like
grandmother's cheeks.

Time breaks open
what was covered

so tightly
underneath youth,

letting go of ideals the
world presents.

It takes courage
to lean into changes,

to let go,
extending time

in each moment
an invitation

to return
to the sweetness of
what awaits.

She Held My Hand

Let the lake tell you my story,
nights spent by the fire
gazing at the setting glory.

Over still waters,
she held my hand,
soaked up tears
eased fears.

Angels

white feather a
gift from angels
found by the lakeside
long ago placed into a
book speaking of
uncertain times.
this morning the
angels found me,
a marvelous prompting
a gentle presence
a surprised falling yet
dancing lightly above
awakening ground
never forgotten, always
protected.

The Hardest Thing

The hardest thing you will ever do...

is
love fully,
dive into unknown waters
have faith the current is on your side,
orchestrating purification
through growth.

is
hold the hand of a
being you love so deeply and
be forced to let go of the
next moment that will be
ripped from you.

is
bear witness to suffering,
yours and mine,
standing in discomfort
fighting for space and

stars to return.

is

stand in your power,

no longer letting

hurricane opinions shame you,

destroy you, pull you up,

as your roots regrow.

is

forgive the paralyzing pain

brought on by another,

guilt of your own doing,

trusting your heart all

over again.

Woody Vine

I stood next to the
woody vine that bends
around another to reach

light.
Skillfully spreading her
roots to water.

Working her miracle
in silence.
Tickles of a squirrel,

affirming
her place in
all.

Time Has Come

Waging war against budding
freedom. How many times
have you settled? been scared? bullied?
silenced? your legs pulled
from your weary body?

Time has come.

Like a white oak,
confide in Mother,
the one who fed you, a
force sustained through time.
Despite all human deeds.

Anchor down.
Breathe, Dear One.

Allow your mind to see
past illusions of control,
forever moving
toward liberation.

Time has come.
Let it be so

Great Spirit

Great spirit circles
   around the same fire,
      phase of the moon,
         heat of the sun.
Promoting everlasting
love evolution.

           Not ever—
             negotiated with fear.

She

Just A Girl

As the candle flickers softly
in a room filled with books
carrying words of many,
she speaks humbly,
grounding softness
into life's journey.

What has brought her here?

Noticing the patterns of
red velvet chairs in which
generations have sat,
she wonders
what her ancestors would say
to the woman

who feels
like she was
just a girl.

She Paused

She paused.

Before she left.

Just one breath.

Closing this door.

To the old life.

So she'd remember.

The difference.

The Turtle

Let me tell you about the turtle.

She loved my yard.
Chose it for her eggs.
All dug up in the dirt.
For the babies she will never see.
For the babies she might never recognize
even as their paths cross in the lake.

She gazed at me with curious suspicion.
A turtle moment later,
she mobilized her body
with determination,
heading towards the unknown to
find a new spot for herself
within the shelter of the woods.

She knew she was entitled to change her mind.

All This Time

Mother Time keeps the girl's pace
digitally, seconds moving,
cells being reborn
spilling wisdom across fields

while skies speak of love
between clouds of sorrow.
She vaguely remembers how
she got here.

Yet with all this time,
she doesn't fret on passing.
Purposefully perfecting her elixir,
grateful for what hasn't changed.

You're Not Your Thoughts

Slow down your reaching.
Give room for change.
Study reactions.
Feel what you feel.
Notice body connections,
not what your
mind has built.

Ego

She liked

who she was.

having met constant change

she sensed a

different version

of her

wouldn't ask permission to unfold.

ego

is

never ready to break.

So she continued.

Living

through

joy and heartache

one

day

at

a

time.

Not Alone

she melts into her own
sacred boundaries,
physical and spiritual,
coming closer to her core,
she discovers
no one is alone.

Shower Yourself

Shower yourself with
attention.
No one is as
special as you.

Nature unapologetically
takes and gives
doing what she knows.
She asks no one.

Neither need you.

Each Undoing Carried No Longer

She resurrected through despair
over and over again.

Each time stripping away a layer
of deception and pain,

Undoing the shackles of plastered
conditioning onto her life.

Carried forward from prosecution.
A spirit's dance,

returning to its wild,
nature,

liberating the authentic.
No longer turning away but

forward.

She Emerged

You can't scare her anymore.
    She walked through the
        valley of death, with nothing but

her bare feet, and the
    crusty salt of tears on her lips.
        As she emerged from the shadows

labored pain, she presented the holy grail—
    to the powers of a perfectly bright
        star-filled sky.

Slow Down

As the bulbs open
deep in the ground
the sun nurtures,
the rain praises.
No attachment—

any single outcome
driven by
higher purpose to
expand and push,
breaking through the

unknown.
The most beautiful
flowers rise as
curiosity dilutes
expectations,

yearning to grow
within this
force,
learning the fine
nuance of what

soul

needs to thrive, which

way heart shapes

individual bouquet.

There is no rush

in creation.

Her Wild Side

Her wild side
dances on abuse,
feet stomping,
hair flinging
into a
surprised wind.

Lifting

Freeing

Oh, there you are.

Deep sigh of letting go.

Freeing breath that

didn't know

was held.

Robins

Joy expands my heart
as a green leaf tip
shows its beauty through
sleeping winter dirt.

First sips of spring,
budding flower,
small dot on the lilac bush
thought dead.

Birds sing a little louder.
Squirrels chase each other
up blooming magnolias.
Meadows open to wildflowers.

Eyes widen, longing
warmth skyward
gazing past
moving time.

I wonder,
if the robins will return,
family from before—

symbol of good luck.

Oh, how I put my intention
to be fortunate again
to listen to their
holy song.

I trust
they will find
the best place to
raise the young.

Just like me,
energy is returning,
after slowing
hibernation,

growing, peaking—
into the world
through a broken
greenish-blue shell.

Fire

Steal the fire.

Bring it home.

When darkness illuminates,

share, but never

ever—

ever, be afraid again.

You are her.

This fire is you.

Lioness

Hurricane for
new soul
initiated,
first breath.
sand erecting
shaping a
majestic
determined
lioness roar.
Blasting away
excess.
Woman
transformed.

Magic

Wandering into thicket
self-loss,
steps turned
against the horizon.
One foot
then the next.

Neglected care,
caring for others'
wellbeing,
opinion,
valued more.

Shame
for straying
off the path
to full embodiment,
striving toward
sense of connection.

No need to be saintly,
but compassionate.

I return to holding
my daughter's hands,

noticing her pulse,
listening to stories about
magic,
believing
      once more.

Goes On

honey toasted sky

lays over the lake

sun rises

two deer carry the world

turtle dives with duck

wild geese echo through

morning mist

squirrels play in

fall painted leaves

nature goes on.

Stand in Whispers

Stand in whispers of noise,
pause, as soul mirror reflects
what exists.

The world wants to be
seen in its miracle.
Light and darkness alike.

Magic illuminates
through the looking glass;
every leaf of grass.

The fox's pray
almost overlooked
in this chaos.

Even through the kneeling
    deep soul struggles,
        pure essence remains.

Motion

Open to the sacredness of not knowing,
bowing into the flow of
endlessly changing commotion.
What was today
can change tomorrow's notion,
exhaustion once more in need of
allowing graceful filled explosion,
proposing openness
towards brave locomotion.

And
then—
you
begin
working
your voice,
building
that dream.
Tracking
through
uncharted territory.

Always forward.
Never back.

Muddy waters
accentuating
your hips.

Gratitude

Gratitude is
anchoring my soul.
People carried,
all the way
through
holding
the torch when
my arms
were too weak,
illuminating
the golden path,
until sight
adjusted.

Insight

Shadows

Not all dark
needs to move to

light. Warrioress
knows both exist.

She stands on
sacred ground,

accepting her shadows, so
others can do the same.

Your Garden

A mindful practice of tending
what is welcome in your garden,
love you want to grow,
seeds you want to sow and
what feeds your soul in the now.

Decide what you desire.
Choose what to plant so
right crops will follow
honesty
a heart fully admired.

You might be afraid
nothing else will show
yet, you stand lonely
tending your hopes
in a one way row.

Sometimes you need to pull all
not to betray
what is bound to fall.
Stop answering the wrong call.

Not all fruit taste the way they claim.
You are worthy of building,
poised love, celebrated,
richness of your fertile soil fame.

In time you will find what flourishes
what has to die
so next season can come
honoring your name.

Life's Loom

Unweaving what has been woven
into unique tapestry
over years takes time.

Not all needs to be
undone.

Divine's creation of
soul's journey
never finished.

Now, every threat needs
consideration.

The pattern will
forever change.
Freedom lives in opportunity.

A cosmic art.
Choose your placement.

You Can't Hide

You can't hide
in the same place

your soul resides.

One Morning

One morning
you will wake and
notice your reflection

mirror in the lake.
Geese carefully watch with
their soft black eyes

tilting their heads
calling for advice. You remember
this repeats every year

a short time all gather here
when season cools the earth
life prepares to rest.

They are not afraid to settle,
befriend the blue heron that
lives life unmeshed.

You notice;
You too returned.

Daring

You must
invite words to
express the
unspeakable.
Release
heavy energies
weighing you down.
Transform the
way you see
the story
you were told is
yours.
Let your voice
birth a free
floating heart of
warrior-ess,
daring to stand
firm.
Calling out
her truth.

I Listen

I am no poet, though
I listen
allowing words to
stream
through the world
like strings of
pearls spun
once
never repeated
unique revelation
released from the
bottom of the sea
rising
into awareness
like rivers,
broadening deltas
fishermen patience—
life comes
unpredictably
as a gift.

What Happens

Raw heartache
braced skin.
One
never fully walks
away
untouched.
Story soaked
karmic memory.
We
collect scars
for all
to witness.
What happens
to one
happens
to
Us.

Attached

Attached to the world through

anything living,

seeking freedom

in promises of love.

some sincere,

others

implied,

amidst

downright lies.

to find

no one can rescue

you

but

you.

Later

When you are little,
the world hovers around the
good or bad.

The nature of mother,
father, devil, god, and
all.

Later you learn,
the world resides in
both shadow and light.

The challenge is to notice
without judgment,
without justification or

a need to be good,
where you belong.

Respectful

Respectfully lift the
rocks of mankind out of
the stream of ancient stories.

One by one examine
the lessons past
leading to present

consciousness
nothing new
under the sun.

Grow brave.
Break free.
Elders' wisdom

guides shield on
exploration of
shun light places.

Empathy

You can have empathy for another's pain

and

refuse to excuse their behavior.

To Craft a Life

To craft a life;
grieve for what was.
walk towards what will be.
root in the now.
marvel in magic.
trust yourself.
transcend into love
despite the promise
that life will
break you.

Masterpiece

I thought I had life
figured out, when
mystery school's
reminder came— connections
come together to part.

Life is art.

Allowing ego to rest,
each day pausing—
universe's delightful stroke,
multitude of color,
unfolding canvas.

Lead with heart.

Surrender to the process.
Everything eventually takes
its rightful place.
Celebrate masterpieces, with
more than one layer.

Love You

Love yourself,
even
when there is
no sign of love.
Love is
you.

Standing

When someone acts and
your heart breaks,
you can look away,
that won't
heal you.

The way through is
attending to what
shattered,
reclaiming power through
softness of

        your feminine soul

           and

        masculine fierceness

             standing in

       truth.

Forevermore

After She Let Go

she noticed stillness in her heart,
as the world around her
carried on.
The honeybees continued
humming the tune of their dance.
Not even her children asked.

And yet, everything changed,
After she let go,

She took responsibility for her own path.
She stopped trying to rescue others.
She learned there are no wrong turns.
She understood what happened was for her.

After she let go
she was no longer a
victim but a survivor.

She unapologetically stepped into her power
no longer awaiting
permission from others.

She realized she is the main character
of this story,
the ones handing her dark plots
her greatest teachers.

After she let go
she let grief soften, not harden her.

She moved beyond
fear to speak up
for her values
rising in authenticity.

She alchemized
pain into generosity as she
warmed her heart on the
flame of gratitude.

She celebrated
she was never alone,
even in the moment when
she broke open.

After she let go, she let it all be, she

invited abundance making the rest of
her life, her best.

Her soul settled into the
woman she has come here to be.
Shining her light—
forevermore.

(inspired by Safire Rose's *She let go*)

Afterword

My hope for you is;

that every single step on your journey through heartbreak will profoundly transform you to your core.
That you will see healing not as a destination but as a
journey.
That you will go deep into a level of your being you
haven't tended to before.
A place where no performance matters and where
you decide your own destiny.

Will you be wounded or awakened?

The day will come when you begin to untangle held
beliefs about yourself that no longer serve you. And you
begin to understand how the world has left deep im-
pressions and conditioning on your way of being that
no longer fit you; places in need of healing.

It won't be an easy path to walk. But the sun will rise
and warm your face. The moon will kiss your forehead
as you sleep, reminding you every night that you are
loved. With each day you will grow more into yourself
and into your new life.

Your expansion will be bountiful. Your body will begin
to feel blissful. Your whole being will sparkle. Your

fierceness will radiate from within. Your mind will sharpen as you reclaim your place.

You will no longer shrink back but become curious about having survived. You will learn to engage from your worth.

Some will try to tear you down coming from their own place of karmic entanglements. Don't get caught up in their vibration. Vibrate higher.

Keep walking.
You are so courageous. Power-full beyond measure.

Let your life unfold. Let go. Surrender when you must. Fight when needed. Inspire others to shine.

Act from love.
Love.
Always following your rising heart.

        ~ from my 🤍 to yours, Ilona

About the Author

Ilona Schenk is an author, psychotherapist, hypnotherapist, and coach who integrates embodiment, writing practices, and grounding through the natural world.
She discovered her love for the power of the written word when her father, a professional bookbinder, brought home book samples as soon as she could read. Throughout her life, she used writing as medicine to process pain and joy.
The intention of her work is to offer the medicine she has gathered from her own journey and through her education. It is her life's purpose to be a guide for healing.
Ilona thrives on helping you see the power you already hold within, claiming your voice, breaking through trauma, and developing courage to authentically live a joyful unique life.

You can find out more about Ilona and her offers at:

www.ilonaschenk.com   and   @ilona_schenk (IG)

If this book touched your heart, please help it reach other hearts.

Consider writing an **online reader review** on the bookseller's website from where you purchased the book.
Your review will support others to choose the book for their own journey.

Freely post **social media** photos of you or others with the book, a poem that touched you, or a picture of the book itself from wherever you are.

Thank you for your support of this book and for helping to spread its healing message.

Kindly include the hashtag
#ilona_schenk   #heartrising